Church Family Camps and Conferences

Elizabeth and William Genné

An Administrative and Program Manual

(Revised Edition)

Judson Press ® Valley Forge

CHURCH FAMILY CAMPS AND CONFERENCES (Revised Edition)

Copyright © 1979
Judson Press, Valley Forge, PA 19481

Library of Congress Cataloging in Publication Data

Genné, Elizabeth.
  Church family camps and conferences.

  1. Church work with families.   2. Church camps.
3. Family—Religious life.   I. Genné, William H., joint author.
II. Title.
BV4438.G46   259   78-24395
ISBN 0-8170-0818-7

The name JUDSON PRESS is registered as a trademark in the U.S. Patent Office.
Printed in the U.S.A. ⊕

DEDICATION

To the First Edition:

> *To Four Good Campers*
> *Nan, Tom, Peg, and Sue*

To the Revised Edition:

> *To the Next Generation*
> *of Good Campers*
> *Desmond, Nelson, Gene, and*
> *Angela Baker and*
> *William Palmer Genné.*

Acknowledgments

As we write these pages, we can see the faces of hundreds of campers who have made these experiences a living reality in our lives. To acknowledge the contributions of all of them would be an impossible task. There is one person, however, whose dedication, expertise, and helpfulness in updating this revised edition have been beyond measure; therefore, we want to say a hearty and public "thank-you" to our friend and former colleague, Ima Jean Kidd, who is the director of the Committee on Outdoor Education and the Committee on Special Education of the Unit on Education for Christian Life and Mission of the Division of Education and Ministry of the National Council of Churches of Christ in the U.S.A.

Contents

Introduction

Family camps and family conferences under church auspices continue to grow. Practically every site or center offers some type of family experience, not only during the summer but also throughout the year. There has been considerable experimentation with a wide variety of ideas. The variety has been so wide that some ideas have been contradictory, and this has created a situation of considerable confusion. Another contributing factor has been the tendency to use the words "family camp" and "family conference" interchangeably.

This book has been written to help churches realize the value in both the camp experience and the conference experience as part of their total ministry with families. Families, as well as individuals, need growth experiences in Christian education.

This book also has the purpose of helping churches think more clearly and distinctly about these two types of experiences and to choose for each occasion the one better suited to achieve the goals and objectives sought. Of course, both the camp and conference as presently conceived allow for considerable flexibility. It is possible to incorporate certain features of each into the other. It is helpful, however, to know which is which.

The FAMILY CAMPING movement owes a great debt to the developments in camping among children and youth. Among the emphases which camping stresses are:

1. The educational value of the real-life situations which emerge when a person or group seeks to live in the out-of-doors.

2. The educational value of a more flexible schedule to permit a full response to these emerging situations.

3. The educational value of the small group in an intimate living experience.

FAMILY CONFERENCES have come out of a different background. Churches in America have long known the "camp meeting," the Chautauqua lectures, the Bible and missions institutes, and similar gatherings which seek to bring together as many people as possible for enlightenment and inspiration and which place considerable emphasis upon teaching and preaching.

In order to handle such large groups, rather elaborate schedules, programs, and forms of organization were developed. Large conference centers were built, with cottages, assembly and dining halls, and planned recreational areas. In recent years, however, in line with sound educational principles, family conferences have tended to limit their size and have included more small group discussion.

This book has been prepared for the family life committees of local congregations and the counterpart state and area committees of denominations and councils of churches in order to help them in the development of their programs for families. It has also been prepared for those selected to give staff leadership to such programs.

As indicated in the text, the sponsoring committee should decide the basic goals and policies of any project and select the leadership for it. Then the leadership staff should develop the program in harmony with those goals and policies. We hope the suggestions that follow prove a valuable resource to sponsoring committees and staffs.

One word of caution needs to be added regarding our fundamental philosophy of working with families. Something of a fad or bandwagon psychology has surrounded family programs as many educational and community agencies, including the church, have come to recognize the primary importance of the family.

Some of these organizations have sincerely developed programs which have been genuine and helpful to families. Others have seemed to exploit families for their own institutional aggrandizement.

Churches have not been competely free from this temptation to institutional self-centeredness. Some have promoted a lot of so-called "family" activity which was really designed to further the institutional needs of the church as an organization.

Other instances have been marked by confusion and unclear thinking. There has been a tendency to label Bible study conferences, missions institutes, leadership schools, and any number of other events as "Family" this or that, when they have nothing to do with family matters.

If a congregation wants to have a supper to discuss its budget and finance campaign, that is all well and good; but it is putting on a "church" supper, not a "family" supper.

If a denomination or council wants to train leaders for its organization or to increase missions giving, it may hold a conference; but it will not be a family conference just because families happen to be invited.

The term "family" should be used to identify only those experiences which are designed to strengthen and enrich family life in its primary relationships.

Recently we were invited to share in the leadership of a so-called family conference. Further inquiry revealed that the primary purpose of the conference was to train leaders for various aspects of the educational program of the churches. Parents spent the greater portion of each day in classes and preparing assignments to earn credits toward a certificate. Younger children were the demonstration students in the laboratory school. Adolescent sons and daughters were housed and fed in a separate area and had a complete, independent youth program of their own. To top it off, it was made clear to us that if we wanted to bring our children, they would have to accept these arrangements. It seemed clear to us that this "family conference" would not be an experience of family living with our own and other families.

To label such a conference a "family conference" seemed to us to border on the dishonest. Let us be honest with our families. They will recognize and respond to the legitimate organizational needs of the church if, on other occasions, the church will recognize their legitimate family needs and minister to them.

The six of us in the Genné family look back to more than thirty years of experiences in living with families in camps or in conferences in Washington, Oregon, Colorado, Wisconsin, Michigan, Ohio, Illinois, Texas, and New York, as well as in Canada, the Caribbean, Micronesia, and Africa. We have seen the growth and transformation that have taken place when a family has found itself in a community of Christian love.

We have seen that wonderful look in the eyes of children who in time of need could turn to any adult who happened to be near with the assurance of a loving response.

We have seen families rise to the crises of illness and accident and, indeed, have seen whole groups of families help each other during epidemics.

We have heard pastors moved to say, "This week has helped my families more than a whole year of my preaching. And it has helped me understand them better than I ever could at home."

Because of these experiences and many others like them, we are firmly convinced and enthusiastically committed to the value of family camps and family conferences as part of the church's total ministry with families. If this book helps to make it possible for families to reach a similar conviction, it will have helped to answer our heartfelt prayer.

ELIZABETH AND WILLIAM GENNÉ

The
Church and Its
Families
1————————

THE CHURCH'S CONCERN FOR FAMILIES

The church and families have been, are, and always will be inextricably intertwined. Jesus was born into a family. His church spread across the then known world from home to home. "The church in your house" is a familiar New Testament phrase. (See Romans 16:5; 1 Corinthians 16:19; Philemon, v. 2.)

The church today, as it faces its mission of proclaiming the good news of Christ, must seek to understand families and to minister to them in such an effective way that each family becomes a channel for the power of God's love in the lives of all of its members.

That families can become channels for God's love is a basic premise underlying the church's work with families. Often the confusions, the perplexities, the failures, and frustrations of family life today tend to overwhelm us to the point of despair. Deeper reflection, however, often discloses the outlines of God's purposes for Christians living in families.

The child growing up in a home is surrounded by others of different ages, different abilities, and different interests. In the midst of the inevitable confusions and conflicts, the child sees the pattern for adult growth in those who are older. Children learn consideration for others, forgiveness, and the true meaning of love—if such characteristics are present in relationships within that family.

All of the modern behavioral sciences are unanimous in their affirmation of the importance of home life in the development of each individual, as well as for the perpetuation of the species and the transmission of culture and values. This does not mean that the influence is always for the good. Those families that are weak or distorted in their relationships may fall far short of a wholesome, positive influence; indeed, the influence may be decidedly negative. Nevertheless, the primacy, intimacy, and importance of such relationships are basic influences, positive or negative, in the development of every person.

This, then, is the reason for the church's concern for and ministry with families. Whether the church's principal task is described as "evangelistic" or "educational," as a "witness" or a "mission," as "liberation" or "salvation," or however else we choose to define it, the fact remains that the church must deal with persons who live in families. The quality of the relationships within those families can be either a tremendous asset to the church in its task or a powerful obstacle. Certainly the church cannot afford to ignore or neglect this aspect of its ministry.

HOW DOES THE CHURCH HELP FAMILIES?

An effective ministry to all persons demands that the church and its leaders must seek to understand the purposes of God in the creation of men and women. Their sexuality, with all its complexities and all its mysteries, must be accepted as part of this purposive creation.

Each woman and each man must be helped to become aware of and to respond to God's love and feel guided in the fulfillment of her womanhood or his manhood according to God's purpose or "vocation" for that person. Thus our churches must minister to those who feel called to remain single as well as to those who feel called to marriage. No congregation should become so "family centered" that it makes the single, the divorced, or the widowed feel left out.

Despite a marked increase in cohabitation without marriage, it is still true that the vast majority of persons marry. These husbands and wives must be helped to have a constantly growing relationship of love for each other, even when they tend to be preoccupied with child rearing. Marriage enrichment, in a variety of forms, has become part of the program of many churches. Many such experiences take place in retreat settings with many features similar to what we shall be describing for families. To help couples keep their love alive and growing from the earliest years of their marriage and on through parenthood and into retirement is one of the basic aspects of family ministries, for healthy families depend on healthy marriages.

Children need to experience relationships in which they are nurtured physically, mentally, and spiritually so that they will have a healthy and wholesome regard for themselves, including their sexuality.

As adolescents, youth need to be guided and inspired as they move out from self-awareness to the establishment of friendships with their peers of both sexes. Whether or not a person ever marries, each person has to learn to relate to, work with, and enjoy acquaintances of both sexes; hence it is important that all young men and women be helped to feel comfortable with each other.

For those who feel called to marriage, the churches must provide opportunities to understand the goals of Christian marriage and the variety of forms in which it may express those goals. The skills of building such relationships as communication, shared goal setting, conflict resolution, forgiveness, and reconciliation need to be developed (not to forget some of the specifics, such as money management, in-law relationships, and proper nutrition and health habits!).

And families, those new unities created by marriage, always need to be guided and helped to recognize their responsibilities toward others in the community and world. Families also have purposes and vocations in God's plans. The family that strives to be strong simply to enjoy itself is in danger of making an idol of "togetherness." Christian families will seek to grow in health and strength in order that they may grow in service to God and the worldwide family.

When the church is willing to give itself in such a ministry to persons where they live, where they suffer, and where they dream, it always finds the loyalty and commitment of a grateful people rising up to strengthen and enrich its life and mission as a church.

In its ministries with families, the church uses many and varied methods, programs, materials, curricula, and experiences. In this book we look at two types of experiences in which increasing numbers of families have become interested and which the church has found increasingly fruitful. These are the family camp and the family conference.

There is nothing in the wide world to prevent a family or a group of families from going off to some resort or on a camping trip entirely on their own without any plans such as are outlined on the following pages. We hope that their church would have given them some convictions and skills that would help them have the richest kind of experience on their own. Some of the resources listed in the back of this book were designed for families "on their own."

The purpose of this manual, however, is to help those churches, denominations, and councils that wish to offer a camp or a conference type of experience as part of a total planned ministry with families. This means that a group of families will go out under church or council sponsorship. To be of greatest value, both to the families and to the sponsor, this experience should be related in a responsible way to the congregation, to the area agency of the denomination, or to the council which sponsors it.

SPONSORING AN EVENT FOR FAMILIES

Many churches and councils now have a committee on family ministries. Sometimes this is a committee with full and regular standing in its own right which includes representatives of the various units of the organization. In a few instances it is a subcommittee of the social service or fellowship department. Often it is a subcommittee of the educational unit of the agency. Whatever its organizational status may be, the unit charged with family ministries should be broadly representative of the total life and work of the church or council. This should be the committee responsible for sponsoring the family camp or conference.

It is the responsibility of this committee to determine the purposes and goals of the experiences it will offer to the families. Once the purposes have been clarified, it can select either the camping type of program or the conference type of program as the better method for achieving its goals. Whether it chooses a camp or a conference will determine the selection of a site, the selection of staff personnel, and the duration, size, and financial arrangements of the event. This sponsoring committee also has the responsibility of promoting the project among its constituency.

Which—a Camp or a Conference?

In the growing movement to minister to families, considerable confusion has developed about the differences between camps and conferences. In the Introduction, we have indicated the divergent backgrounds out of which the two types of programs developed, and we noted the camping emphasis on experiences in the natural environment to enhance self-understanding and interpersonal relationships. The inspirational teaching emphasis of the conference tends toward a more cognitive experience, although in recent years these distinctive emphases have tended to merge in some aspects of their programs. Some conference-type programs have been held on campsites. Elements of camping programs have been developed within conference programs. Likewise, elements of conference programming have been used in some camps. Some sponsors have even used the hyphenated term "camp-conference" to describe their program. How can we distinguish between the two?

A conference may be held on a campsite, but it could, insofar as its program schedule and activities are concerned, be held just as well at a resort hotel, a college campus, or in some similar setting. The out-of-doors is integral to the camping experience.

A conference may include some appreciation of God's out-of-doors and some skills in outdoor living, but these are not as essential to the daily living routines as they are in a camp.

Both the family camp and the family conference are concerned with the strengthening and enrichment of Christian living within the family, but their methods and emphases vary.

In order to decide whether to use a camp or a conference, the responsible committee of the sponsoring agency will want to consider carefully the descriptions of the camp-style and the conference-style experiences outlined in the following two chapters. The committee must also consider the needs and the readiness of the families in its constituency. It should keep clearly in mind the goals of Christian family living fostered by its church or agency. Then, in the light of these goals and needs, committee members should formulate the specific goals and objectives for their project and select the type of experience they consider better suited for their purpose.

SUGGESTIONS REGARDING PROMOTION

The announcement and promotion of either a family camp or a family conference will be quite similar. Therefore, before moving to a consideration of the details of organization and program, we make the following suggestions regarding publicity which will be applicable to either.

The sponsoring committee, in consultation with the camp or conference director, is responsible for promoting the event.

Timing the announcement is very important. If summer vacation dates are involved, the announcements should be ready by the first day of December of the year preceding and certainly not later than the first day of January. The need for this is obvious: work schedules must be cleared months in advance, and the family will want to coordinate this event with other summer plans. Even weekend projects in local congregations need to be announced early enough so that all family members can clear their schedules.

Purposes should be clearly stated in all publicity. Since family programs are a new experience for some, explicit interpretation is required. Family camps or conferences are not simply cheap vacations, nor are they military camps where everyone is routed out at the crack of dawn by a sharp blast from the bugle. They are not events to which the wife and kiddies go while father goes fishing or golfing. They are opportunities for whole families to grow together as they live with other families in a Christian community.

The most effective publicity is person to person. In a local congregation, the sponsoring committee should carefully arrange personal contacts with as many families, including the children, as possible in addition to general announcements and printed or mimeographed materials.

Committees serving groups of churches in synods, conferences, or state or provincial organizations should try to arrange a presentation to interested persons, preferably by families who have already taken part in such a program. In inaugurating the first event, it is the responsibility of the committee to lend its personal support in this kind of face-to-face presentation. Once the program has gotten under way, families from one church will usually be willing to visit other nearby churches.

While general announcements have some value, presentations should be made to specific groups, such as adult classes, women's societies, men's clubs, couples' clubs, and, of course, parent study classes.

Family events should be presented in a separate and distinct leaflet which describes the event's values, objectives, and activities. General announcements of children's and youth programs cannot be expected also to carry the interpretation of the family programs, although family events may be listed there.

The leaflet should be either printed or mimeographed and should be attractive and illustrated, if possible. It should be designed to answer all (or most!) of the questions each member of the family may have. It should include:

1. The purpose of the event, concisely stated.

2. The place, with description of site (pictures or drawings, if possible), clear directions for travel, mail address, and phone number.

3. Dates, with specific arrival and departure times.

4. Sponsoring agency and address.

5. Director's name and, if known, other staff.

6. Costs—the date the enrollment fee is due, the date the balance is due, and a listing of "extras," if any.

7. General description of the program and the minimum ages of children welcome.

8. Information regarding health and safety certification and practices.

9. A list of what to bring: amount and type of bedding, clothing, other equipment.

10. Enrollment blank with space to list parents' names; children's names, birth dates, and grades in school; address; phone number; and, if necessary, home church and pastor's endorsement. Enrollment deadline date should be clearly indicated.

Such leaflets should be placed in the hands of parents or mailed to them individually with letters of invitation.

Visual aids are a potent means of promotion, especially when movies, slides, or pictures of actual family programs in progress can be shown. To promote the first event, visual aids can usually be borrowed from some nearby agency. Pictures of the living accommodations, dining hall, and waterfront are most influential in bringing about enrollments.

Early enrollments may be encouraged by having a cheaper registration fee for those who enroll before a certain date. A deadline of four weeks prior to the date of the event should be set to encourage early decisions. Refunds can be made in case of illness or other family emergencies.

The enrollment blank should be returned to the director-family or forwarded to this family at once upon receipt in the sponsor's office. As soon as the enrollment is received, a process of communication should begin which can be vital to the success of the project.

The directors will want to send immediately a word of greeting and some word about their own family (perhaps even a snapshot) and enclose a "family portrait sheet" (see Appendix D) for the family to return. This initial letter should be personalized. If mimeographed, it should provide for personalized salutation and signature and for some comments, for instance, that there are children of the same age in the two families.

If there are young children in the enrolling family, an additional sheet may be enclosed giving information about food for youngsters, high chairs, whether cribs are available, provisions for laundering, and similar information.

After the family portrait sheet has been returned, the directors should note the interests and abilities of the various family members. The directors may write asking them to bring some special craft or hobby equipment or to share in the leadership of the camp in some particular way. (Caution: While it is good to involve new people, some check should be made on their abilities before committing critical responsibilities to them.)

About a month or three weeks before the opening date, the directors should send a second letter (see Appendix C) to all enrolled, giving the names of the other staff families, confirming the time of the opening day (especially when the first meal will be served), and enclosing a suggested schedule for at least the first twenty-four hours. Information about where to report upon arrival and the procedure regarding health checks should also be included in this letter. If cabin or room assignments can be made in advance and a map of the site enclosed, interest will be heightened.

Some directors like to suggest that the family prepare a distinctive sign to be placed outside its cabin or tent. The children can often think of colorful, pictorial signs, such as "The Byrd's Nest," "The Hutchinson's Hutch," or "Our Jackson's Hold." Usually such signs include figures and names for each family member so that passersby will get acquainted with all the family members.

Some directors like to suggest that during the trip each family compose a jingle or song to be sung the first night. For this, some have used:

> Hi Ho! Hi Ho!
> It's off to camp we go,
>
> _____
>
> _____
>
> Hi Ho, Hi Ho!

Throughout all these preliminary communications, the joy of living and sharing together in this kind of experience is kept uppermost. It should be made clear that, while the schedule will be very relaxed and leisurely, the event will nevertheless be an adventure in personal and family growth and that everyone will be expected to share in the leadership at some point.

Families who feel a personalized interest from the time they send in their registrations will be the best promotional agents for the following years.

Planning for a Family Camp

2

PURPOSES AND GOALS

The first national consultation of governmental and private agencies interested in family camping defined such camping as follows: "Family camping is an adventure in outdoor living. The family exercises its ingenuity in providing shelter, preparing food, and enjoying the natural environment."

Christian family camping is all this and much more! To paraphrase this definition, we might say: "Christian family camping is an adventure of living in God's out-of-doors. The family exercises its ingenuity in providing shelter, preparing food, and enjoying the natural environment to the end that all family members may have an increased awareness of God as Creator and of his love as revealed in Christ. Through their shared activity, they become aware of the meaning of Christian cooperation and community and are better able to express these values in their family living."

Some of the values of family camping have been described in the following contrasting statements:

1. Family camp helps us to realize our dependence on nature. We become ecologically aware of the sources of food, water, atmosphere, and the other life-sustaining parts of our ecosystem.

2. Family camp helps us to realize our independence. We can simplify our life-styles and develop survival skills without depending on things and gadgets.

3. Family camp helps us to realize our dependence on each other. Responsible cooperation and teamwork are essential.

4. Family camp helps us to realize our independence as we develop our own resourcefulness and confidence in outdoor living.

5. Family camp helps us realize the value of simple, communal life.

6. Family camp helps us realize the inadequacy of a life concerned with only the physical necessities.

While keeping these basic definitions in mind, the sponsoring committee will need to remember that family camping may be conducted in a variety of ways. Families with children approaching adolescence or older who have experience in outdoor skills may want to backpack or canoe in the wilderness. Other families, less experienced and with younger children, will do better with a cabin as the base for their out-of-door explorations. In some tent or recreational vehicle areas, families will cook all their meals. At other developed campsites there will be a central dining hall for most meals, with cookouts arranged as they are desired.

The sponsoring committee will need to make its decisions in the light of its purposes and with due consideration of the needs and readiness of its families. If it decides on a camping experience, the committee will need to locate an adequate site.

STANDARDS FOR SITE, FACILITIES, AND EQUIPMENT

Local congregations may use their denominational camp properties or any accessible state, provincial, or national parks. YMCA, YWCA, or Scout campsites are often adaptable to family camping if their basic facilities can meet the standards. Camps that have cabins for six or eight campers can usually be adapted to family camping by assigning one family to each cabin. Barracks-like cabins or dormitory sleeping rooms are not suitable for families. Nor is it sufficient to hang a blanket or curtain between families. The basic requirement for a family campsite is that each family have privacy for its sleeping arrangements. Families may share dining facilities and sanitary facilities, but each family needs and deserves a place of its own in which family members can dress, sleep, and have the opportunity for discussions in private.

The sponsoring committee should use the checklist in Appendix B to evaluate the physical facilities, living accommodations, food service, and sanitary and health facilities of any campsite under consideration. The checklist is based on the standards of the American Camping Association and the Committee on Camps and Conferences of the National Council of the Churches of Christ in the U.S.A.

DURATION OF STAY, SIZE OF GROUP, AND COST OF PROGRAM

The length of time is an important element in the educational experience of any group. For families from the same congregation who already know each other, a well-planned weekend can be a very rich experience, but a whole week together would multiply the benefits. When families come together from an area representing several local communities, five days should be regarded as a minimum. A full seven-day week would be preferable.

A local church could sponsor a weekend with three or more families using their own recreational equipment, either tents or vehicles. Ten or a dozen families would constitute an ideal size for a camp. To exceed a maximum of twelve couples, including the leader families, would create problems that impair the efficacy of the experience.

It is important that all members of the family household participate in the camp experience. This policy should be firmly adhered to. Fragments of families or part-time participation are not good for the family and disrupt the camp morale.

A minimum age for children should be agreed upon and clearly stated in all announcements and publicity. Our present knowledge and experience would indicate that camping activities are beyond the physical endurance and maturity level of children under five years of age. Families with children under five should be referred to a family conference or invited to wait until their children are five years old.

Financing a family camp will need the careful attention of the sponsoring committee. Because of each family's need for privacy, cabins cannot be filled as efficiently as when occupied by sex-segregated groups. Economic considerations should never be allowed to destroy privacy.

If the sponsoring agency is convinced of the value of this kind of experience, it will also make sure that any family, regardless of its size, is able to take advantage of a family camping event. Some camps in both the United States and Canada have established a flat "family rate" regardless of the size of the family. This tends to insure the attendance of the total family unit. Some congregations also make scholarships available to families of limited means to insure that a representative cross section of all families is included.

Some camps have a sliding scale of fees, graduated according to adults, teenagers, and children under twelve. Others use a consumer cooperative plan, charging a fixed fee for certain fixed costs and then sharing only the actual costs of food and other supplies.

Of course, in local church camps, the committee may provide the program expenses while each family brings its own food and shelter, either tent or recreational vehicle.

If necessary, the sponsoring agency should try to arrange some subsidy for the family camp in order to keep the cost within the reach of all. In camps serving a large area, often the local church will pay up to half the cost for each of its families. This has been found to be a good investment because families usually come back with increased vitality and interest in the work of the church.

It should be unnecessary to add that careful records should be kept and sound financial procedures followed regarding purchases and the payments for expenses. Insurance for campers should be arranged if it is not provided by the management of the site used. Agreements with site managements, staff, and any related personnel should be in writing.

STAFF PERSONNEL

Depending on the size and location of the camp, staff requirements will vary greatly. Three or four families from a local congregation may wish to administer their camp and program through informal cooperative committees.

A larger group may wish to secure the use of an established camp that already has its own qualified staff for cooking, dishwashing, maintenance of buildings and grounds, and supervision of the waterfront. In such an instance, the group would need only to provide the program staff for its own activities during its stay. If, however, the group is "on its own," it will need to see that maintenance tasks, meal preparation, cleanup, sanitation, and so on are provided for.

Let us assume that the staff for the physical plant and functions of the site are provided for in a way that meets the legal requirements and the best standards for such operations, and let us turn our attention to the program leadership. There are four basic requirements which should be regarded as absolute minimums for all leadership:

1. An understanding of the commitment to the Christian way of life. Occasionally, families of a different faith may be included for some specialized assignment (for example, a Jewish family to help us understand the Jewish faith and family customs, or a Muslim or a Hindu family to help us understand its culture), but even in such cases the camp should clearly reflect Christian values and concerns for family relationships.

2. An understanding of the dynamics of family life and the ability to demonstrate those understandings in a successful family.

3. A personal maturity, making it possible to work with others at a deep level with a minimum of friction.

4. A commitment to a philosophy of leadership that believes in persons and seeks to release their potentialities for continual growth.

The leader families in a camping experience function largely as resource persons; as enablers helping each family or small group of families to plan, to enjoy, and to grow in a variety of projects, such as nature hikes, beach walks, cookouts, out-of-door crafts, and through the routines of daily living. The leader families are participating members of the group, living with the group throughout the duration of the camp. They help the others gain skill in a variety of activities and share the leadership with them. At appropriate times they also help them gain insight into their family interactions. Basically they aim to make Christianity a living quality in all activities and relationships.

Leadership for the family camp must be very versatile, combining skills for outdoor living with real insights in the application of the Christian faith to the everyday interactions of daily living within each family. The sponsoring committee should make every effort to secure and, if necessary, provide training experiences for the best leadership available.

PROGRAM PREPARATIONS

Once the sponsoring committee has determined the policies outlined above and the director-family and the leader families for each group of families have been selected, these families will be responsible for making preparations for the program and guiding the experience of the camp.

Preplanning Session

The budget should include provision for the staff families to assemble for a day together as soon as the leadership roster is known. Certainly this should be at least a month before the camp and at the site, if at all possible.

After learning about each other's backgrounds and interests, they should get acquainted with the site, either by direct inspection or by having a full description of the facilities and resources with which they will have to work.

Next they should look at the portrait sheets (see Appendix D) of the families enrolled. Families can then be assigned to "colonies" or "communities." These are groups of three families who will be together throughout the camp, sharing in the planning, work, recreation, and worship as a unit. Each group of families includes a leader family.

Families with children about the same age might well be grouped together. Families with younger children should be placed closer to the toilets. New families might well be mixed with the more experienced campers.

If the portrait sheets reveal certain special interests, these might also be taken into account when grouping the families into colonies.

Certain activities will usually be coordinated with the total camp group, such as meals (if a central dining hall is used), swimming, and evening get-togethers for parents after the children have retired. These can be agreed upon by the leader families working together as a team and in consultation with the manager of the camp property.

The next step in the preplanning session is to review the purposes and goals as they have been stated by the sponsoring committee. Perhaps the staff families will want to modify or stress some particular aspects of the purpose in the light of the situation in which they will be working or the families which will be attending. The purposes and goals should be so well understood and agreed upon that they become the motivating force for the whole leadership team.

Following the precamp planning session, each staff family should begin to assemble resource materials and outline program possibilities. Any supplies should be ordered in ample time for delivery to the site. Correspondence might be opened with those families who will be in the colony.

All leader families should plan to arrive on the site at least the day before the session begins, if not forty-eight hours before the opening. This will allow time to get comfortably settled and to explore the site if this has not been done before. That evening the leader families can develop the schedule for the first twenty-four hours and check on any final details. They also need to have some recreation and worship together. They should be physically rested and spiritually poised to greet the camper families when they arrive.

A Good Beginning

Everything that happens in camp from the moment of arrival until the family departs is part of the camp experience. The alert staff, therefore, will be "on their toes" (in a relaxed manner, of course!) to provide a good beginning. Some provision should be made to cover the following:

1. A greeter near the entrance to welcome families and to direct them to the registration center (and, if desired, to the toilets).

2. A registration procedure as efficient and expeditious as possible to: (*a*) assign cabins or sites for tents or trailers, (*b*) collect fees if not

previously paid, (c) refer families to the health center, and (d) perhaps provide a beverage and a cookie.

3. Health check by a physician or registered nurse. If local regulations do not require a health certificate of examination, there should be at least a "3-T Check" of temperature, toes, and throat.

4. Guides to cabins or tent or trailer sites. Children of the leader families may serve as guides. At least one parent of the leader family should be in the colony area to assist families in getting settled. Note: All this may be done on an informal friendly basis without necessarily labeling the leader family. A community of helpfulness should be developed but without too much dependence on a designated "leader."

5. Activities. Of course, families will want to get settled. They may be provided with materials to make signs or name tags if they have not made them before. Provision should be made for a refreshing swim and orientation to the aquatic program or an exploratory tour of the site, if time permits.

If a central dining hall is being used, the evening meal should be announced well in advance to give families ample time to find their way. (See dining room suggestions on page 41.)

The first evening's program can be announced at dinner and should be leisurely enough to allow folks weary from traveling to find their way in new surroundings. If an evening vesper service is to be a regular feature of the daily schedule, it would be good to introduce it the first evening.

During the remainder of the first evening, the colony group may have its own campfire, get acquainted with each other, and begin to discuss some of the possibilities of the week.

The next morning after breakfast, worship, and cleanup, the total camp assembles. There can be a get-acquainted session. One device sometimes used is to have the fathers stand in a circle, with their wives in front of them, and the children in front of the wives according to size. Each family radiates like the spoke of a wheel, and each family can see every other family as a unit.

After the basic structure of the program, such as mealtimes, swim times, and other total camp activities, has been agreed upon and the necessary work routines and assignments have been established, there can be a general description of some of the possibilities of the week.

Despite the preparatory materials which each family previously received, the director-family should interpret once more the purpose and spirit of the camp. This should be done with depth of conviction and a joyous feeling of adventure in Christian growth. Some folks will surely be skeptical and others may be scared. Help them relax in the accepting and supporting atmosphere of Christian fellowship.

✓ Avoid "rules and regulations." Whatever rules are necessary may be presented informally as the understandings we need to have so that we can all live together in safety and harmony.

✓ Avoid harsh-sounding commands. Instead of "Report at nine o'clock sharp," try using, "Let's gather together as promptly as possible at nine o'clock. We've got a lot of interesting things to do."

Various activities may then be described, and any special opportunities in connection with the campsite or the nearby area can be mentioned.

Following this total camp assembly, the colony groups can move out together for a more extensive exploration of the campsite. In any hiking or exploratory activity, the colony should move together for two reasons: new discoveries can be shared, and it also prevents anyone from getting lost.

Each colony may begin to make plans to improve its area. Tables and other conveniences may be needed, and these can be constructed in good camper fashion out of the materials at hand.

If the colony is housed in cabins or recreational vehicles, the families may want to develop a "home-in-the-woods" where they can meet comfortably and possibly build their own campfire circle, fireplaces for cookouts, and such other conveniences as may help them enjoy their time together.

Other special events, such as cookouts, hikes, or nature wonder walks, may be worked into the plans. Special types of collections—rocks, driftwood, and so on—can be considered. Bird-watching or star-gazing and other special nature interests may also be planned. Perhaps there is some ecological project to improve the campsite that can be worked on.

It will be impossible to do everything; so the colony families will need to begin to select those activities in which they are most interested and to block out their time. Each day they will need to plan activities for the day. Some time should be devoted to the completion of projects already begun. Other time can be used to start developing activities to satisfy interests not yet met. Always the plans should be kept flexible to meet changing weather conditions and other emerging situations.

Building a plan day by day, a colony might have a schedule by the end of the week that indicates the use of the major blocks of time as shown on the chart which follows. This schedule was the creation of one colony. The schedules of other colonies in the same camp varied considerably from this.

	Sunday	Monday	Tuesday	Wednesday	Thursday	Friday	Saturday
M		planning	build	breakfast	nature	hike	commu-
O			home-in-		collec-		nity
R		explore	woods	cookout	tions		cleanup
N		site	fire-	planning			
I			place			lunch-	
N		choose home-				out	
G		in-woods					
A	arrive	rest hour	rest hour	rest hour	rest hour	swim	closing
F							evaluation
T	get	campcraft	finish	swim	prepare		
F	settled		fireplace		cookout		leave
R		swim		prepare			
N			swim	campfire	cookout		
O				for			
O				whole			
N				camp			
E	vespers	vespers	colony	campfire	colony	colony	
V			vespers	with	vespers	camp-	
E	colony	colony	and	other		fire	
N	campfire	campfire	fire	colonies	games		
I						vespers	
N							
G							

Moving On

As the colony begins to roll on its own momentum, the members of the leader family should be especially alert to certain elements in their experiences which they can use to enrich the camp. Many opportunities to observe the dynamics of family interaction will come as parents and their children move from activity to activity throughout the day. The leader family should note the evidences of cooperation, helpfulness, support and trust, forgiveness and love. Some of these can be mentioned in informal conversations or in the parents' get-togethers around the evening campfires or perhaps, if appropriate, in the worship experience.

Of course, as in any new situation (and in too many old ones), there will be some evidence of tension, pressure, and other less desirable qualities. In one camp, a father who was a production engineer was constantly pressuring his son to "get a move on" as they were setting up their tent. Finally the leader asked him quietly, "What are you hurrying for? Do you think you're still moving the assembly line?" When the father realized his habitual on-the-job tenseness, you could almost see him begin to "unwind." He was a different man by the end of the week, and he and his son were getting along much better.

One of the real opportunities of family camp is to develop better communications between teenagers and adults. By assigning youth to dining room teams and other committees where they can work with adults not their parents, opportunities for new insights can be developed.

As the colony members become acquainted with the habits of various birds and animals, they will see running through nature many evidences of God's plan and provision for his creatures to have homes and families. Biologists used to think of nature's "law" as the survival of the fittest, and poets would claim that "nature is red in tooth and claw." We now know that there is a delicate and intricate balance in nature and that survival goes to the most cooperative.

As we become more aware of these various ecosystems and our dependence on them, we begin to see how precious clean water, clean air, and nutritious food are. In the camp setting it is natural to discuss the need to simplify our life-styles and eliminate our wastefulness of some of these precious resources.

When families begin to feel the orderly rhythms, the beauty, and the fundamental goodness of nature, a deeper spirit of serenity and goodness begins to flow through their lives and a new quality is introduced into their patterns of daily living.

Many of these "wonder-full" experiences will provide the natural occasion for worship, and families should be encouraged to express their feelings spontaneously and creatively. Most groups like to have a vesper service each evening at which time either the colony or the camp as a whole can lift up in worship some of these experiences. Vespers should be family planned and directed.

In addition to grace at meals, there should be a time each day when families are encouraged and helped to experiment with their own family devotions. Leaders should see to it that some of the resources of their denomination or some that are listed in the bibliography of this manual are available. Many families trace their observance of family worship to their first experiences in family camp.

As families increase in their awareness of God, they will often want to explore his word in the Bible. Some time may be allotted to Bible reading and discussion as a colony in addition to the worship experiences.

Music in worship and in general fellowship should be one of the features of camp. It is one of the "naturals" for carry-over value into the home activities of families. Our family has had many happy times and has covered many miles singing the songs we learned in camp.

Music should run like a thread throughout the days and activities of camp. Many table graces might be sung. Even the younger children can join in singing graces, such as the following (both sung to the tune "Old Hundredth"):

> Be present at our table, Lord,
> Be here and everywhere adored;
> These mercies bless, and grant that we
> May spend our lives in serving thee.

> Lord Jesus, be our holy Guest,
> Our morning joy, our evening rest,
> And with our daily bread impart
> Thy love and peace to every heart.

Other singing in the dining room should be carefully, if subtly, supervised. Loud, boisterous songs have no place at mealtime in a family camp with so many younger children. If some of the quieter fellowship songs are sung, it should be after the meal is finished.

There are many other opportunities for music and singing. Work songs can be sung while doing chores. Walking and hiking songs can accompany these activities. Songs from other nations can be real introductions to other cultures. Many contemporary songs carry real spiritual messages. Carefully chosen hymns can enrich vespers. A good camp is a singing camp where music may burst forth spontaneously at any time.

An Effective Closing

As the camp moves toward its conclusion, it should move toward a climax, a culmination of the spiritual impact on each family. A variety of closing programs has been used, and new variations and combinations are constantly emerging. Some effective programs have been:

1. A Family Fellowship Circle. The members of each family join hands, making a small circle. First each family faces inward on itself,

thanking God for the experiences of the camp. Then the members face outward, joining hands with all the other families and pledging themselves in service to others. Prayers may be interspersed with hymns that have become meaningful during the camp.

Such a circle makes an effective closing after the last meal, just before departure. (Remember the children; don't make it too drawn out.)

If families have been saving their money during camp for some gift of sharing, they may bring their gifts to the closing circle.

In some camps, a spokesperson for each family makes a brief statement about the family goals which have grown out of the experience.

2. Closing Worship. Sometimes the closing evening's vesper service has been made the high point of the camp. In one camp, each person brought some special symbol of the whole camp experience, often some piece of craft work or some bit of nature that had been collected during the camp.

3. Camp Covenants. The leaders of many camps have felt it of value to suggest that families set down in permanent form some of the resolutions they have made as a result of the camp experience. This has been done in various ways. (a) A statement has been formulated by a representative committee gathering up some of the great themes of the experience together. In one camp, an artistic member illuminated the text and all of the family groupings signed it. Each family was provided with a copy (see Appendix E). (b) Some families have written themselves letters which were left with the director-family, who mailed them about January 1 of the following year. (c) Other families have simply written out the statement they read at the closing fellowship circle and have kept it as part of their own camp mementos.

However it is done, some opportunity should be given to families to think clearly about the implications of the kind of living they have experienced in camp for their daily living at home, and they should be encouraged to plan some practical next steps to carry the values of the camp experience back into their homes. Whether or not any public record is kept or word expressed, families should be encouraged to acknowledge that the experiences of camp were a reality and a clue to what might become real in their own home lives.

An Evaluation and Follow-up

While the experience is fresh in the minds of the participants, it is good to get them to evaluate the program to guide the sponsoring committee and staff in making plans for future camps.

One camp gives each family an evaluation sheet that can be discussed in the "family talk time." Each family hands the filled-in form to the director-family as they bid others good-bye at the gate the next morning.

The evaluation sheet need not be complicated. Questions like the following may be used:

> What did you (like most)
> (find most helpful) about camp?
> What suggestions do you have for our next camp?

More elaborate checklists might be used with ratings for various aspects of the program, but these are seldom necessary. Campers are usually a very outspoken lot!

Be sure that the children's evaluation comments are included in the written responses. These can be very enlightening.

An evaluation session by the leader families is of great value. If it can be arranged for them to stay over for a period after the campers leave, they can give their own evaluations while they are fresh. After this is done, a review of the campers' recommendations may be made. Recommendations to the sponsoring committee can grow out of the staff and camper evaluations. This should be done promptly to help the sponsoring committee in its planning for the following year.

Many camps have had a follow-up in the form of a reunion in the fall following a summer camp, especially if the camp is sponsored by an area presbytery, district, or conference. Such a reunion is usually spontaneously suggested by campers who feel "we must get together sometime!" A reunion has a twofold advantage: (1) it provides another type of evaluation by the very attendance and the reminiscences, and (2) it helps in promoting interest in future camps.

A reunion may be simply arranged. A centrally located church can invite the group in the fall. The campers may bring their lunches, or they may be served a meal if advance reservations are made.

Usually they come to the Sunday morning worship service of the host church. After lunch they show snapshots and slides of the preceding summer's camp and report on some of the things the families have been doing or thinking since summer. Camp songs may be sung, and a brief camp-style worship service may conclude the afternoon's fellowship.

If the sponsoring committee can announce the dates and the leadership for the next camps, that helps to increase the momentum of the interest of the campers.

Some new families may be invited to the reunion to learn about family camp, but too many "prospects" change the dynamics of a reunion into a promotional event.

The focus of the reunion is not so much nostalgia for the past summer as a chance to continue the process of growth begun at camp.

Where a reunion does not seem feasible, clusters of families within traveling distance may be encouraged to visit each other.

Planning a Family Conference

3

PURPOSES AND GOALS

A family conference is somewhat like a honeymoon. It is an experience in a new setting, free from accustomed responsibilities and routines, during which the persons involved can devote their time and attention to establishing newer and more satisfying relationships in the light of their Christian commitment.

Unlike the honeymoon, however, the family conference involves a group of families living, working, studying, playing, and worshiping together in a common quest to understand more fully and to demonstrate more clearly the power of Christ in their family living.

Attempting to gather these thoughts in a more precise definition, we might say: "A Christian family conference is an experience of living in a community designed to help each family respond increasingly to God's love as revealed in Christ. Through shared work, study, play, and worship and with the guiding and supporting fellowship of the church, the participating families seek to grow in the understanding and practice of Christian love."

The sponsoring committee will need to make its decisions in the light of its own purposes and with due consideration of the needs and readiness of the families. If it decides on a conference experience, the committee will need to locate an adequate site.

STANDARDS FOR SITE, FACILITIES, AND EQUIPMENT

A conference, like a honeymoon, will probably be helped by beautiful natural surroundings. If the committee is inclined to consider a campsite for its conference, it will want to be sure to read what was said about sites in the preceding chapter on camping.

A conference, however, may be held at a resort hotel, a college campus, or some other similar conference center. In any event, the committee will find the checklist in Appendix B helpful.

DURATION OF STAY, SIZE OF GROUP, AND COST OF PROGRAM

In any educational or growth experience, the length of time is an important factor. A local congregation, whose families already are well acquainted, can sponsor a well-planned weekend that will be a very rewarding experience. A full week together would multiply the benefits.

Conferences, sponsored by some synod, diocese, or other area organization which bring strangers together, should be very carefully planned if a weekend is the only time available. Many planning committees consider five days a minimum time and feel that a full seven-day week would be better.

A local church could sponsor a weekend conference with three or more of its families. One church reserved all the rooms of a motel during an off-season weekend and held discussions in the parish house of a nearby church. On Sunday morning the participants joined with the local congregation in worship.

Many facilities can accommodate thirty, fifty, or even more families, and it is always a temptation to try to bring together the largest group possible for reasons of both economy and eagerness to reach as many families as possible. We were in a conference once that enrolled fifty families, totaling over 160 people. While the conference was not without some value for those who attended, the large numbers tended to overstimulate the children. The teenagers tended to gang up and go off on their own. Even the parents tended to fragment into a number of small groups, usually based on their friendships prior to camp. This tendency toward cliquishness left out some of the newcomers and impaired the movement of the whole group toward unity.

If the members of the conference planning committee should find themselves overwhelmed with increasing numbers of families registering, they could arrange to divide the families into colonies or clusters of five to ten families each. The program for the conference would include the community building within these clusters.

Our present knowledge of sound educational procedures and our experience with groups would indicate that a group of twenty families should be considered maximum. This would mean between eighty to one hundred persons. To exceed this maximum would create problems that even the most careful planning could not eliminate.

It should be firmly stressed, however, that all members normally residing in the household should participate in the conference. It enriches the whole program if another generation, like grandparents or other relatives who may be living in the home, is included. Foster children are a very real part of the family living; so they would, of course, be there. If the conference is to lift the level of family living, this can happen much more readily when all who live together share in the experience.

It is important that the age of all who attend should be such that they are not too much of a burden on the other members of the family. Experience has indicated that children under four should not be included in the family conference. Their participation is limited, and they limit participation of other members of the family. This policy should be clearly announced in all presentations or publicity so that there will be no misunderstanding.

Financing a family conference will need the careful attention of the sponsoring committee. Because of each family's need for privacy, living accommodations usually cannot be filled as efficiently as when occupied by sex-segregated groups. Economic considerations should never be allowed to destroy privacy.

If the sponsoring agency is convinced of the value of this kind of experience, it will also make sure that any family, regardless of its size, is able to take advantage of a family conference. Many conferences have established a "family rate" regardless of the size of the family. This tends to insure the attendance of the total family unit.

Some conferences have a sliding scale of fees graduated according to adults, teenagers, and children under twelve. Others use a consumer cooperative plan, charging a fixed fee for certain fixed costs and then sharing only the actual costs of food and other supplies.

Local churches may use some of their education budgets or special funds to provide leadership for their conferences, leaving the families to cover the living expenses. Congregations often share in the costs of sending their families to conferences sponsored by synods, districts, or other denominational agencies.

Careful financial records should be kept, and sound procedures followed regarding purchases and payments for expenses. Some type of insurance coverage should be arranged. Agreements with site managements, staff, and any related personnel should be in writing.

STAFF PERSONNEL

Depending on the size and location of the conference, staff

requirements will vary greatly. Three or four families from a local congregation may wish to administer their conference through informal cooperative committees, perhaps depending on their pastor as their principal resource person.

The quarters for larger conferences usually have their own qualified staff for cooking, dishwashing, maintenance of buildings and grounds, and supervision of the waterfront. In such an instance, this group would need only to provide the program staff for its own activities during its stay at the site.

Let us assume that the staff for the physical plant and functions of the site are provided for in a way that meets the legal requirements and the best standards for such operations, and let us turn our attention to the program leadership.

The four requirements we listed as basic for camp leadership on page 24 also apply to conference leadership. Briefly stated they are:

1. An understanding of the commitment to the Christian life,
2. An understanding of the dynamics of family interaction,
3. A personal maturity and ability to work with others,
4. A commitment to shared leadership that releases potentialities for continual growth and leadership in others.

The leaders of the conference should have a basic concern to see that Christianity becomes a living quality in all of the activities and relationships within the family. In the conference type of program, however, leaders will function somewhat more like teachers. Of course, the leader family will share as participants in all of the activities of the conference; its leadership will probably be in a particular area of preassigned responsibility. The leader family may be responsible for conducting parent discussions on family relationships or the activities for children or youth during designated periods.

The program staff of a family conference can be kept to a modest number. Many responsibilities can be carried forward by families or committees, reducing the need for invited staff. When leader families are invited, often the different members can carry different specific responsibilities in accordance with their talents and interests. For example, a father may lead the children's activities, the mother may lead the parent discussions, and a son or a daughter can coordinate the craft activities.

The following functions or areas of responsibility will need to be provided either by staff invited for the specific purpose, by designated families from among those planning to attend, or by committees made up of individual members of several families:

1. GENERAL ADMINISTRATION. Codirectors, usually a lay couple, have general oversight and administration of the total program. It is preferable to avoid the academic formality suggested by the title "dean."

2. WORSHIP. This is usually planned by a committee. The pastor or some clergyperson may be invited to bring the vesper messages, but others should be involved in the conduct of the services. This committee is also responsible for arranging grace at meals and for making suggestions for individual family worship.

3. DISCUSSIONS FOR PARENTS. Such discussions may be organized by a committee, but more frequently they are assigned to a specially invited resource leader.

4. ACTIVITIES FOR CHILDREN AND YOUTH. When age-segregated activities seem desirable, leadership may need to be provided at several levels, according to the age distribution. (See activity suggestions on page 45.) Usually such activities are directed by invited leadership.

5. HOBBIES AND CRAFTS. Usually these are coordinated by one person, assisted by various delegates who share their skills with others. If the conference is in an out-of-door setting, nature appreciation and some skills in outdoor living may be included in these activities.

6. MUSIC. One or more delegates may have responsibility for leading the singing for fellowship and worship.

7. RECREATIONAL ACTIVITIES. These are usually organized by committees of conferees according to their interests.

It is also desirable to arrange for the attendance of a family representing another nationality or race, or a missionary family, who can help the other families appreciate the wider horizons of the Christian experience.

It is the function of the sponsoring committee to see that leadership for these functions is the best possible. It should feel a responsibility for making training experiences available to potential leaders.

Once the sponsoring committee has determined the policies outlined above and the staff has been selected, the codirectors and the staff are responsible for planning the program of the conference.

PROGRAM PLANNING
Preplanning Session

The budget should include provision for the codirectors to assemble the staff families for a day together as soon as the leadership roster is known. Certainly this should be at least a month before the conference and on the grounds where the conference is to be held if at all possible. In addition to this preplanning session, the staff families should arrive on the site at least twenty-four hours before the conference begins.

In the preplanning session, after learning about each other's backgrounds and interests and their assigned responsibilities, the staff members should get acquainted with the facilities in which they will be working, either by direct inspection or by having a detailed description.

Next they should look at the portrait sheets (see Appendix D) of the families enrolled. If any special interests or circumstances are revealed, these should be carefully noted.

Living accommodations can be assigned by the codirectors, keeping the families with younger children closer to the toilets and mixing new families among those with previous experience.

The next step in the preplanning session is to review the purposes and goals as they have been stated by the sponsoring committee. Perhaps the staff members will want to modify or stress some particular aspects of the purpose in the light of the situation in which they will be working or the families which will be attending. The purposes and goals should be so well understood and agreed upon that they become the motivating force for the whole leadership team.

By the close of the planning session, the staff families should have an understanding of each other and of their specific responsibilities and be ready to function as a team—one for all and all for one—as they carry forward the program.

Following the program planning session, each staff family should begin to assemble its resource materials and develop more detailed program plans. Any supplies should be requisitioned in ample time for delivery at the conference. Correspondence should be opened with those families who might be asked to assume special leadership responsibilities.

A Good Beginning

Plans will need to be made for the following:

1. A greeter near the entrance to welcome families and to direct them to the registration center (and, if desired, to the toilets).

2. A registration procedure as efficient and expeditious as possible to (a) assign living accommodations, (b) collect fees, (c) refer families to the health center, (d) perhaps provide a beverage and a cookie.

3. Health check by a physician or registered nurse. If local

regulations do not require a certificate or examination, there should at least be a "3-T Check" of temperature, toes, and throat.

4. Guides to living quarters. Often children of staff families like this assignment.

5. Activities. Of course, families will want to get settled. They may be provided with materials to make signs and name tags, if they have not made them before.

A supervised play area might be provided for the little ones while the parents are getting settled.

Provision should be made for swimming or an exploratory tour of the grounds, if time permits.

The directors should plan to tell the families about the first meal well in advance in order to give them ample time to find their way to the dining hall.

Dining Room Suggestions

There should be a supervisor in the dining hall. One of the staff should be chosen well in advance of the first meal to take on this important assignment.

At many conference centers, the conferees have only to set the tables, serve the food from a counter to the tables, and clear the tables following the meal.

The staff supervisor should organize the teams of servers. Sometimes the various teams will each serve one meal in turn. Other conferences have each team serve the three meals for one day. Teams are made up of one member from each family to equal the number required to provide a server for each table. Each team usually has a leader who acts as the supervisor for that meal.

Seating is very important in a family conference. If there is no plan, families with small children often get separated and there is general confusion and scrambling for seats.

One plan that has worked well is for the dining room staff supervisor to prepare a large name card for each family and indicate on it the number in the family and the number of children needing "assist" chairs. She or he then works out the combinations of families that will fill each table. Tables should not have more than eight places. By placing the cards on the tables, the waiters know how to set them. When the families arrive, they can look for their place cards, knowing they will all be able to sit together without a breathless scramble. By shifting the combinations of cards, various families can get acquainted. Some conferences like to shift the seating at each meal (which usually means that the same combinations will sit together several times during the week). Others like to let the same combination of families sit together a day at a time.

Sometimes at luncheon, all the teenagers might be allowed to sit at special tables.

If the management of the conference center likes to place the dessert on the table at the beginning of the meal, the person in charge should be reminded that, with younger children attending, this should be avoided.

The atmosphere in the dining room should be kept quietly relaxing, and care should be taken that younger children do not get overstimulated at mealtime. Children seven and over can be assigned to waiter teams as helpers, with due care taken about their handling heavy or hot serving dishes. It must be made clear, however, that only the serving team should move about during the meal. Otherwise this can create considerable confusion.

If songs are sung, they should be of the quieter type and should not begin until the tables are cleared. Announcements should be kept to a minimum.

The First Meeting

The first meeting is very important in setting the mood for the week. Depending on when the conference begins, it may be planned for the afternoon or the evening. Some simple get-acquainted mixers are desirable as soon as the families begin to assemble. When most of the group has arrived, some group singing is always appropriate. Then it might be well to give the whole group a chance to introduce themselves as families, giving the names and ages of the children.

Care should be taken during this get-acquainted time to avoid status symbols. Leave off titles and do not ask for occupations. Let nurses and bankers, teachers and farmers, plumbers and lawyers mix without labels. When in the course of the conference they do discover what each does, they may be in for some wonderful surprises.

Despite the preparatory materials which each family previously received, the directors should interpret once more the purpose and spirit of the conference. This should be done with depth of conviction and a joyous feeling of adventure in Christian growth. Some will surely be skeptical and others will be tense. Help them to relax in the accepting and supporting atmosphere of Christian fellowship.

Avoid "rules and regulations"; these can be presented informally as the understandings we need to have so that we can all live together in safety and well-being.

Avoid harsh-sounding commands. Instead of "Report for

classes at nine o'clock sharp," try using "Let's gather together as promptly as possible at nine o'clock. We've got a lot of interesting things to talk over."

Draw the families together with a contagious enthusiasm rather than by the exercise of authority. In most of the conferences in which the authors participate, we make it quite clear that only one thing is "required": conferees do not have to come to meals, but they must observe the rest hour after lunch!

During this first meeting, the program can also be reviewed and schedules distributed, if they have not been sent in advance. Any necessary work routines and assignments can be established at this meeting.

Have the first meeting so well planned that there will be no fumbling around or lost motion, yet make it look as relaxed as a leisurely conversation. Give folks the idea that something real is going to happen every day of the conference, and they will not want to miss a session.

If it is an evening session, it would be good to bring it to a close with an informal period of "coffee, cocoa, and conversation." Some of the most valuable sharing of experiences comes during these evening snacks.

In family conferences there need not be a formal "lights out" time, but everyone should be encouraged to get adequate rest for the full day ahead.

A Typical Time Frame

The staff should work out the proposed schedule for the conference. This will be subject to review and adaptation by the conference council. It may be changed or varied as the activities progress. Such a schedule might look somewhat as follows:

7:00 A.M.	Rising
7:45 A.M.	Breakfast (morning devotions at table)
8:30 A.M.	Housekeeping
9:15 A.M.	Age-level activities for children
9:15 A.M.	Parents' Bible study or chaplain's hour
10:00 A.M.	Parents' discussion of Christian family life
11:00 A.M.	Family hour: hike, swim, projects
12:15 P.M.	Luncheon
1:00 P.M.	Rest hour
2:00 P.M.	Quiet projects, crafts, etc., for those awake
3:00 P.M.	Family hobbies, sports, swimming, etc.
5:45 P.M.	Dinner

6:30 P.M.	Family fun and informal games
7:15 P.M.	Individual family worship
7:30 P.M.	Vespers
8:15 P.M.	Bedtime (for juniors and younger)
8:45 P.M.	Parents' evening program (teenagers with parents or in own group)
10:00 P.M.	Fellowship snack (coffee, cocoa, and conversation)

Basic Principles of Scheduling

Keep the schedule leisurely—

toddlers take time;

housekeeping by families takes time;

besides, it's vacation!

After-dinner activities may be adjusted in order to take advantage of sunset at vesper time.

Regional variations should be kept in mind (for example, in the warm Southwest, hikes and other physical activities should be scheduled in the cool of the morning).

Keep all schedules flexible enough to meet changing circumstances (such as weather) and interests of the group. Each conference can shift the time in response to the expressed needs of the conferees, the council, and the staff. The daily schedule may be changed for a special program event or sessions combined by mutual agreement.

The staff will want to plan some opportunities for the parents to think together about Christian family life and nurture in the home. These may be provided by having age-segregated periods during the morning, as in the schedule given earlier, or by having the planned discussions in the evening after the younger children have gone to bed. Evening sessions have the advantage of allowing the parents to be with their children throughout the day, but they have a disadvantage in that the parents are rather weary by the close of the day.

Even when there are morning sessions for parents, sometimes one or two evenings are given over to the presentation of movies or plays dealing with family situations. These can be discussed over the coffee or cocoa until bedtime.

One of the real opportunities of a family conference is to develop better communication between teenagers and their parents. By assigning youth to dining room teams and to other committees (sometimes even asking their leadership to chair the committee) in which they work with adults other than their parents, opportunities for new insights can be provided. An excellent morning or evening discussion can be developed with both teenagers and adults in the same session. Another suggestion is to show a family movie or read a play and then divide the teenagers into small groups with adults, not their parents, to discuss it. Both teens and parents have spoken enthusiastically about the value of this type of discussion. Talking together as youth and adults without the emotional involvements as family members is often helpful.

Many conference staffs are now planning a series of intergenerational sessions in the schedule. If some of the conference families are living with three generations in the home, this age range of experience and wisdom can be used as a dimension of enrichment for all the families there. We are discovering anew the value of intergenerational sharing and education.

Other topics that frequently recur in the interests of parents are: discipline, understanding child development, resisting community pressures, developing community responsibility, handling hostilities, wise use of time and money.

Many of these lead right into questions of choice and the moral basis on which we make choices. Matters of faith are directly involved; therefore, ample time must also be allowed for the specific discussion of faith. This may be done by scheduling a special period to deal with Bible study or questions of a more specific religious nature. Some conferences work this material in with the other developmental questions, using the same leadership. Other conferences may develop a dialogue between a family life consultant and a clergyperson, each bringing out the respective aspects of the same questions.

Youth Fellowship

The number and variety of youth activities at a family conference should be planned in accordance with the number in that age category who are present. All sons and daughters older than high school age should participate in the adult discussions. If there are fewer than eight of high school age, they, too, can readily be absorbed into the adult discussions.

If there are about ten or more young people who are in the seventh to twelfth grades at school, the staff should consider whether it would be wise to plan for some special activities for this age group.

A leader should be provided for the youth who can meet with them while the parents are having their discussions. He or she can use some of the youth responses on the portrait sheets (see Appendix D) as a starting point. Young people of this age are often interested in vocational choices, and the inspirational character of the family conference is a good background against which to consider such choices.

If there is a family of another race or nationality in the conference, the family group may be invited to meet with the youth for a session or two.

The youth leader should keep in touch with the leader of the parent discussions; and when both groups are ready, they might merge for one or more sessions to discuss the relationships of teenagers and their parents.

During the evening discussions, the youth might well be included with the parents. The teenagers may, however, prefer to spend one or two of their evenings pursuing their own interests.

It is always good if one leader can meet with the youth throughout all their separate sessions, even though other guests may be invited to speak on certain topics. The continuous leadership develops a rapport with the young people, and the leader is better able to develop experiences of growth as well as experiences of understanding and communication with parents.

Certainly the teenagers should be appointed along with adults to all of the work teams and conference committees. This shared responsibility for the total conference enterprise is most valuable.

Occasionally the youth fellowship as a unit should undertake some responsibility on behalf of the total conference. It may, for instance, work with the waterfront director in organizing and conducting a water carnival for the conference or plan some other kind of recreational event. The youth may also help to conduct one of the vesper services.

The major emphasis should be on participation in the family activities of the conference. The youth fellowship should not become self-conscious or overactive to the point where its activities interfere with the total family activities.

Children's Activities

The conference staff will also need to plan the activities for the various age groups of children for that portion of each day when age-segregated activities seem appropriate. Some folks are so family centered in their thinking that they regard any age-segregated activity as a violation of the spirit of family programs. Anyone who has ever lived in a family, however, knows that there are certain times of every day when adults pursue their own interests while the children play with others of their own age. This rhythm of activities for children and youth does not seem to us to violate the spirit of family living which recognizes the developmental needs of the various members as long as the major portion of the day's program offers activities to the family as a unit.

Since, in the conference setting, you cannot simply send the children "out to play" and since the age-segregated activities also provide a valuable opportunity for helping the various age groups "respond increasingly to God's love as revealed in Christ," age-segregated activities ought to be carefully planned as a vital part of the total conference experience.

The variety of activities that could be done with boys and girls depends on the amount of time at your disposal and on the setting for the conference. If there is a two-hour session in the morning, it can be broken into periods for some discussion, some project activity, some recreation, and some worship.

If a theme for the week is selected, it will help the children to tie together their experiences. A leader for each age group, qualified and experienced in working with children, should be designated. An assortment of books on various topics can be made available for children to use during their quiet hours. It is always wise to have some movies on hand—particularly those dealing with animals and wildlife—to use especially if the weather prevents outdoor activity.

If the conference is held on a site where some nature study is possible, the interest in the outdoors and in families can often be merged into a series of activities for junior-age youngsters such as the following. The theme used here is "God Has Provided Homes."

Session I

Topic: How God's plan provides a home for every living thing—a home best suited for its needs.
Discussion: After getting acquainted with the boys and girls, discuss the various kinds of homes we know about.
Activity: After discussion and browsing through several nature books, decide on some animal for special study. This study may include: (1) making a diorama of the home of an animal; (2) making a three-dimensional picture showing the cross section of a home, such as a beehive, wasp nest, or beaver dam.

Session II

Topic: Different kinds of homes.
Discussion: What different kinds of homes do living things have?
Activity: Take a walk and write down all the homes you see (it is well

to have at least one magnifying glass for each four children). After the walk, compare notes and make a composite list (using felt-tipped pen on large sheet of paper). Also start gathering material for the major project you will make.

SESSION III

TOPIC: Adaptation to environment.
ACTIVITY-DISCUSSION: Have children bring to the group anything they have caught (frogs, worms, insects, etc.). Discuss how to care for these until they are returned to their homes at the end of the session. Study adaptation devices—webbed feet, gills, eyelids, etc. List on a large sheet: "Things I Learned Today."

SESSION IV

TOPIC: Protection afforded by homes.
DISCUSSION: How do various types of homes provide protection and suitable environment for young until they can take care of themselves?
ACTIVITY: Continue to work on the major project selected during first session.

SESSION V

TOPIC: Homes for growth according to God's plan.
DISCUSSION: Reports on homes built in major projects and on how they provide for security and growth for the inhabitants.
ACTIVITY: Compose, as a group, a litany of thanks to God for all the homes in this world. Arrange for an "open house" so others can see all the group has discovered.

With the increasing discussion on ecology and the importance of our learning to know and care for the world, there are splendid materials available in books, filmstrips, and movies that could be used either with the children or with the whole conference.

Throughout all these discussions, parallels can be drawn to the care, protection, and nurture of human families, and insights can be gained for mutual helpfulness in the home. For younger children of the primary age, a series could be developed showing how all living things grow according to God's plan.

Family Activities

The conference staff should allow the major portion of each day for activities by families. In addition to eating and sleeping, there should be adventures in worship, crafts, recreation, discussion, and decision making. While the initiative and integrity of each family need to be respected, the staff will need to provide leadership and supervision for some activities, such as swimming, while for others, the staff will need to provide resources to assist families, as in learning new crafts.

In the schedule suggested earlier, note that the eleven o'clock hour in the morning is a family hour. Swimming is usually the principal activity of this hour, although some families will take walks or spend their time in other ways as they choose. Usually there are no special offerings of crafts or games at this morning hour since the families are encouraged to function on their own initiative as units.

The afternoon, following the lunch and rest hours, should be kept perfectly free for families to engage in whatever activities they wish. If the activity area is close to the sleeping area, the activities from two o'clock until two-thirty or three may be restricted to the quieter crafts in order that the younger children may enjoy longer naps. Some conferences call this the "tiptoe hour."

CRAFTS. One of the prime purposes of the family conference is to knit the family members together with an increasing number of activities they enjoy doing together. If the conference is in an out-of-door setting, nature study, nature crafts, and collections would be a "natural." It is also valid to help the families gain some skills in crafts they can share together in their homes throughout the year. Jewelry making with shells and beads, leather craft, banners, macramé, and a host of other hobbies can be introduced to families. Whittling and making willow whistles and pinecone figures can be special delights if the natural materials are available.

Some conferences insist that at least one parent work with each child on a craft so that it becomes a shared skill or interest in the home. If the whole family can agree to explore and develop a craft together, so much the better (and the process of decision making may prove to be the most valuable part of the whole experience).

The conference staff should designate a craft coordinator. He or she can use the portrait sheets to determine those crafts in which there is most interest and also whether there are among the conference families some who are willing to take the leadership in sharing a craft skill with the rest of the group. It helps to suggest that a leader share his or her hobby for only two or three days so that he or she can use the remaining days to be free to explore new crafts with his or her own family.

The craft coordinator should be responsible for ordering all the necessary craft supplies. He or she may ask various families to bring the supplies for their specialties, but he or she should estimate the probable demand to keep the costs of supplies within budget limitations.

In planning for crafts, it is good to offer some simple things in which the younger children can share as well as those requiring more skill for more advanced persons. Something like clay modeling using a pottery clay that needs no firing can be used by children but can also be worked into more elaborate forms by adults.

Leather working also may begin with simple do-it-yourself kits, which give youngsters some real satisfaction, but might also include some advanced tooling designs for those with more experience in working with leather.

Emphasis should be on the enjoyment of self-expression and shared enthusiasms rather than on technical perfection. Any exhibits should include the work of all, including the youngest. Do we need to add that there should be no competition or prizes?

RECREATION. While recreational activities will usually be under the direction of a committee of the conferees, the staff will want to do some advance planning to insure adequate use of the facilities of the conference site and to make sure that the necessary equipment is available.

The emphasis should be on the simpler and less expensive forms of recreation which families can enjoy together, such as hiking, beachcombing, bird-watching, swimming, etc. Sometimes segments of families may enjoy a sport together, as when a father and son comprise a doubles team for tennis, or when husband and wife pair off for badminton (parents have a right to enjoy themselves together!).

Sports in which only one member of the family is active should not be given any time in the family conference schedule. Elaborate tournaments and competitions are to be avoided. In one conference, two fathers played off the Ping-Pong singles championship at 1:30 A.M. of the closing day of the conference. This kind of buildup of pressure in the schedule is inexcusable.

Spectator sports should also be avoided. This may be difficult because of the widespread tendency toward this type of activity. Many parents actually must be taught how to *play with* their children. Left to their own devices, they may never adopt a family hobby or learn any new skills together or even enter into the family games. The recreation program at a family conference is, therefore, a serious matter. Through it families learn techniques and resources to carry over into their home life.

Play activity is important for another reason. A family conference is usually a vacation time for most of the families. It ought to feel like a vacation, with plenty of fun and relaxation. Experience shows that it is unwise to shortchange this fun feature.

Those who lead the recreation should be skillful and patient in helping grown-ups and children play together. Simple rhythmic games and folk games with songs that accompany them are fun for most families.

Swimming should be available in summer family conferences if at all possible. The recreation committee should have a subcommittee to help the waterfront director, but each family should be charged with the primary responsibility for its own members.

If there is to be instruction given in swimming and other skills, it is always better if parents can be helped to teach their own children. Any approach that helps build the ties between parents and their children should be explored.

Talent nights are questionable if they tend to show off only one member of a family. It is better to have a "Family Fun Night" stressing the participation of all the family members.

Caution should be exercised in the development of the recreation program. It is not wise to pack into one week all the games and sports a committee can think of. Families should not return home worn out. It is especially important to avoid overstimulation of children. Recreation should always be regarded as a means toward Christian fellowship and not as an end in itself.

MUSIC: Music has one of the greatest possibilities for carry-over value into the home activities of families. Our family has had many happy times and has covered many miles singing the songs we learned in family conferences.

Music should run like a thread throughout the days and activities of the conference. The first song in the morning might well be a hymn of praise played on a trumpet or over a loudspeaker.

Many table graces might be sung. Even the younger children can join in singing graces, such as the following, sung to the tune "Old Hundredth":

> Lord, gratitude we offer all
> Who labor that we may be fed;
> O bless us as we work for them,
> Bring kinship through our daily bread.*

* See other grace suggestions on page 31.

Other singing in the dining room should be carefully, if subtly, supervised. Loud, boisterous songs have no place at mealtime. If some of the quieter fellowship songs are sung, it should be after the meal is finished and the tables have been cleared.

There are many other opportunities for music and singing. Work songs can be sung while doing chores. Walking and hiking songs can accompany these activities. Songs from other nations can be a real introduction to other cultures. Carefully chosen hymns can enrich vespers.

Guitar accompaniment can add a great deal to group singing, whether it be at the table, around campfires, at evening meetings, or at vespers. In the letter of welcome to the conferees, you might invite families to bring guitars, recorders, and other musical instruments to be part of the music at the conference.

A good conference is a singing conference where music may burst forth spontaneously at any time.

WORSHIP. During the family conference, many families will begin experimenting with new forms and ideas of family worship (many for the first time!). In addition to the opportunities offered by the conference schedule, the staff should plan for adequate resources and for some guidance to assist those families that want help.

Denominations that use liturgical forms of worship will find the family conference an excellent opportunity to acquaint families with their forms for family worship and to enrich their understanding of the stated hours for daily observance.

In addition to the corporate experiences of worship for all the families at the conference, there should be opportunities and encouragement for individual families to worship as units. In many conferences, if there are sound amplification facilities, a family may conduct table devotions in a way that is genuine worship in its own right but also serves as an example of what might be done by other families.

The early morning watch, so popular in youth conferences, is hardly applicable to the family conference because of the younger children. The children do not prevent some conferences, however, from scheduling a period of meditation during which families can begin the day with prayer together.

By far the most popular time is the vesper service after the evening meal. This can be either the highest point or the lowest point of the day. In far too many cases, it is the latter. When the service is too long and too dreary and does not communicate, it is indeed unfortunate, because not only it is unpleasant, but it also teaches all the families that corporate worship by families is to be avoided.

The conference staff should plan to work with a worship committee of the conferees to see that the services are brief, resourceful, and with real meaning to the whole family. The leadership of the services should include campers of various ages who can read Scripture and lead in prayer. Simple music, rightly used, can enrich the services.

One of the most effective series of vespers related each service to the period of individual family worship which immediately preceded vespers. At the close of dinner each evening, a text or a question was given for the families to consider in their devotional period. As the family gathered for worship in its cabin or out under a tree, the family members discussed this question and then moved directly to the vesper service, where the question or text was developed more fully. For families who have never tried or experienced any kind of devotions or meditations in the home, this plan was helpful.

Many conference staffs have found it valuable to prepare mimeographed guides for the periods of individual family worship. Denominational family devotional guides are often selected. Families usually need some specific helps to get started in this practice that is new to most of them.

Table grace is another place where many families need help. Many conferences provide a little card for each meal on which is printed a grace that can be read or sung together. At the close of the conference, each family is given a packet of these cards to take home.

The Sunday morning worship service in a family conference differs little from vespers, except that it may include a special offering for some cause selected by the families and it may include some special music. The important factor is that the whole family can worship together regardless of ages. For this reason, the service should be brief and interesting, even to the younger children.

An Effective Closing

The suggestions made in the preceding chapter regarding the closing of family camps (page 31) are also appropriate for family conferences. The conference staff should begin in the earliest planning to consider the kind of climax toward which it wishes to move. Although this may be modified during the course of the conference, it will be valuable in providing a sense of direction.

An Evaluation and Follow-up

The conference staff should plan from the beginning for some kind of evaluation and follow-up. The simple evaluation suggested in the preceding chapter on family camps can easily be adapted to the goals of a family conference. The suggestions regarding follow-up are also applicable to a family conference.

Final Preparations

All staff families should plan to arrive on the site at least a day, and preferably two days, before the conference begins. This will allow time to get settled and to explore the facilities, if this has not been done before. That evening the staff families can check on final details and also have some recreation and worship together. They should be physically rested and spiritually poised to greet the families as they arrive.

Once the conference is under way, the plans described earlier can be carried out. It is valuable for the leadership staff and the committee chairpersons to meet briefly each day to coordinate plans as they are developed by the committees and to modify previously made plans as may be necessary.

In some conferences, the codirectors create a family council composed of one member from each family. (In one, it was suggested that each family with children over twelve send the child who was closest to twelve years of age. Families whose oldest child was younger than twelve were asked to send either the husband or the wife. By this plan, the council represented a cross section of age and sex as well as each family in the conference.) The council receives the suggested schedule and activities from the staff and committees and acts upon them. The council can also initiate its own ideas for the good of the conference. Each council member is encouraged to discuss the ideas with his or her own family. This stimulates the processes of discussion and decision making within each family.

Areas
of Concern and
Opportunity
4 ───────────

In any congregation there are families with special needs: the widowed, the orphaned, the divorced, the separated, and those who have members who are physically and mentally handicapped. The ministry and fellowship of the church must embrace and sustain them in the name of our God who loves the last, the least, and the least attractive. Committees on ministries with families should be especially alert to make sure that these families also have some opportunities for appropriate camp or conference experiences.

One of the things such families need most is a loving, accepting, meaningful association with other families. However, incorporating certain types of families into an ongoing camp or conference requires a special alertness on the part of the leadership and the quality of concern in the conduct of the program. In our list of resources are special materials to help committees and staffs incorporate such families in camping and conference experiences.

Resourceful and imaginative families with special needs are finding that in many activities they go far beyond the limits they originally anticipated. It is the responsibility of our churches and agencies to stimulate, encourage, and support these explorations and to help these families grow in self-reliance and the fullness of life as they respond to God's love.

Parents Without Partners

Most fathers or mothers who are trying to go it alone have developed a self-reliant attitude. Some who have been recently bereaved or divorced may still be struggling to gain an emotional and spiritual equilibrium. The experience of the camp or conference may be exactly what they need at this critical juncture of their lives.

To be alert to their needs does not mean to make a fuss about them or to pamper them. It is always better to treat them on the assumption that they are capable of assuming their responsibilities as parents and participants.

Children who are hungry for a missing parent will often, and quite understandably, attach themselves to the mothers or fathers of other families. Other parents who observe such a fixation might quietly arrange also to befriend the child. This will relieve the first "foster parent" of some of the responsibility and let the child know that he or she has more than one friend.

There is a nationwide association of fathers and mothers who are rearing their children without a partner. Many of the local chapters of this organization have been initiated or aided by church leaders. This association sponsors an interesting variety of educational and recreational events. Further information can be obtained from Parents Without Partners, Inc., 7910 Woodmont Avenue, Washington, DC 20014 (phone: 301-654-8850).

Families with Handicapped Members

In recent years a number of specialized organizations have been developed to help families who have a member handicapped by blindness, hearing deficiencies, mental retardation, or crippling diseases. The National Council of Churches has developed a Committee on Special Education to help the denominations include such persons in their programs. This committee's directory of resources is included in our bibliography, and further information can be obtained from the committee by writing Room 708, 475 Riverside Drive, New York, NY 10027.

It is the responsibility of the church to call specialized agencies to the attention of a parishioner who needs them. It is also the responsibility of the church to work with such agencies to help meet the deepest spiritual needs of the families they serve.

However, whenever possible, these families should be included in the church-sponsored events along with other families. This will require considerable grace (using that word in its highest spiritual meaning) and skill on the part of the staff leadership.

The staff members should check their own attitudes about such a venture. Have they the patience and love required by the special needs of such families? Do at least some of the staff have some experience and insight in working with the particular difficulties involved? What special problems might the site, facilities, and the program pose for a family with a handicapped member and how will they be solved?

The invitation to families with handicapped persons may have to be specific and direct, on a person-to-person basis. If the parents have tended to become ingrown because of feelings of guilt and shame, it may take a bit of special effort to make them feel genuinely welcome and accepted. Even though persons are oversensitive or self-conscious about their handicaps, however, it should be made clear from the very beginning that, in the main, families with a handicapped member are going to be treated as every other family and that they will be expected to fit into the activities and responsibilities.

The staff will need to set the mood and spirit which will guide the other families in understanding and accepting the family with the handicapped member. The basic principle to be kept in mind here is that each one of us, even the so-called "normal" person, has certain strengths and certain weaknesses. These weaknesses may be considered our "handicaps," but we learn to live with them and not to let them get us down.

In much the same way, members of a family with a more severely disabled person must be helped by real experience and fellowship to live with their handicap. With the loving, but at the same time challenging, support of a group of Christian families, many families with handicapped children have been helped to a newfound freedom which has made possible amazing growth for both parents and children.

The presence of a family with a handicapped member is often one of the most powerful dynamics in the camp or conference experience. All the families will grow in understanding and compassion. Children will often have their first encounter with a person so limited. The whole setting adds a depth to the meaning of Christian community.

Three-Generation Families

In both camps and conferences, it has been the policy to urge the entire household that normally lives together to participate. This would include grandparents, maiden aunts, bachelor uncles, or any other relatives or foster children living in the household.

Grandparents can often be helped as much as parents by the experience of living with other families under the inspiration of a Christian fellowship. They gain some insight into the dynamics of family interaction and may gain some objectivity as they live with other families.

There is a further advantage to having some grandparents

present. In our time, mobility and many other factors make it impossible for some children to know their own grandparents well. Many children will "adopt" grandparents, and so older persons may find themselves surrounded by many who are not their direct descendants.

Older Couples

With the increasing attention focused on persons in retirement and the older years, we have been forced to be concerned about their family relationships. We have discovered that many of these couples have livelier interests and greater capabilities than we have ever imagined. Conferences especially focused on older couples have proved immensely worthwhile, although their inclusion with families of other ages should be promoted wherever possible.

The same procedures outlined earlier can be followed in developing a conference for older couples. The schedule will need to have a more leisurely pace, but you can be sure to count on some lively discussions.

One of our happy recollections is a camp for "over 65s." They had a merry fiddler in their group, and their square dance was one of the jolliest we have ever attended.

OTHER TYPES OF FAMILY EXPERIENCES

Churches are showing increasing imagination and ingenuity in using some of the natural interests of families as vehicles for strengthening and enriching the quality of Christian living within those families. There are many varieties of experiences which the alert church will seize and transform to help in the nurture of its families. Space will permit us only the brief mention of four types of projects on which there has been scattered experimentation in recent years.

Family Tours and Caravans

With vacations on wheels becoming increasingly popular, some churches are organizing family tours and caravans. Several families with their own recreational vehicles cover a route together. They visit religious and historical shrines and places of scenic beauty along the way and plan to stop together each evening. Often they visit home mission projects, church colleges, and other churches, which make the work of the church in the world today come alive. Some of the experiences of living and traveling together make the caravan seem like a camp on wheels. Many of the suggestions about planning a family camp are applicable to planning for a family caravan.

One Michigan church found ten of its families planning trips to the Rockies. With some advance planning, they agreed to converge on Yellowstone Park on a certain date and spend a week together. They had the shared experience of seeing the awe-inspiring wonders of the park and of camping together for the period. This kind of fellowship makes for real enthusiasm in the ongoing work of the church, as well as providing intrinsic benefit to the families involved.

Trail, Canoe, and Boat Trips

Some families with adolescent children like to backpack or burro-pack into the wilderness. Others like to use canoes or boats as their mode of transportation. When churches find some of their families engaging in such activities, it is time for these churches to ask, "How can we help our families get the most out of these experiences?"

One church developed a year-round interest group on camping. Meeting monthly throughout the winter, the members compared notes on equipment, trails, and places to see and experimented with camp recipes. Their meetings included family singing, games, and worship. By the time they hit the trail in the summer, they were already a well-seasoned crew.

Groupings by Vocation

With the increasing concern in our churches about the ministry of lay persons, especially in relation to their vocations, some churches have turned to the family conference as an ideal method for dealing with some of the problems uncovered. It is well known that certain types of work place greater stress on families. The church can bring together these families who are in the same predicament and help them. Some of the families who have been helped by such conferences are those of armed services personnel, persons whose jobs require extended travel or even residence overseas, physicians, clergy, and teachers.

Families of any workers who face unusual hours or working conditions may need the help of the church. Certain professions involving intimate contact with the opposite sex or involving secret or confidential work have their own particular problems. If the gospel of Christ is to become relevant in the lives of these people, it must be a saving and healing force at these very specific and difficult points.

Work Projects

Family camps and conferences have been challenged by some who feel that they make an idolatry of family togetherness in a world that is sick and torn and bleeding. Such folks insist that Christian families should manifest more sensitive concern for a wider humanity.

These persons claim that a Christian family conference becomes most effective when families cease being concerned about their internal relationships and unite in a common effort to serve some area of need.

With this in mind, the American Friends Service Committee and a few other groups have built into their family conference programs work periods during which all the families build a playground in a depressed area or rehabilitate a community center.

Such experiences have indicated a positive experience for families. A word of caution needs to be added, however, to remind us that a *family* work camp needs to keep its primary focus on the quality of the interaction within the family and to help the family grow in its understanding of Christian values and witness.

The temptation to exploit family labor simply to develop a church camp or conference site must be avoided. The study and discussion periods that characterize all good work projects should be concerned with the impact of the experience on family values and behavior.

Resources
for Program
Building
5 ————————————

Good leaders will bring to any program their own rich backgrounds and personalities and will use a variety of resources in their own unique ways. For church-sponsored events, it is always wise to check with your denominational publishing house for resources. The following are suggested because of their proven value. The prices listed with the resources are subject to change.

ADMINISTRATION

Church Camping, Robert P. Davis. John Knox Press, Atlanta, 1969 ($3.95).

Church Camping, Robert P. Davis. John Knox Press, Atlanta, 1969 and South America, 10 E. 79th Street, New York, NY 10021, 1978 ($1.00).

Directory of Resources for Outdoor Education. Committee on Outdoor Education of the National Council of Churches, Room 708, 475 Riverside Drive, New York, NY 10027, 1977 ($1.00).

Family Camping: Five Designs for Your Church, John D. Rozeboom. United Methodist Church, Discipleship Resources, P.O. Box 840, Nashville, TN 37202 ($1.00).

Site Selection and Development: Camps, Conferences, and Retreats, Maurice D. Bone *et al.* United Church Press, New York, 1965 ($12.50).

Strategic Planning for Church Organizations, Richard R. Broholm. Judson Press, Valley Forge, 1969 ($1.00).

Toward Excellence in Church Camping. United Methodist Church, Discipleship Resources, P.O. Box 840, Nashville, TN 37202 ($1.00).

Also from United Methodist Church, Discipleship Resources:

Camping with Retarded Persons ($1.10)
When You Go Canoe Camping (75 cents)
When You Go Trail Camping, Wallace E. Chappell (75 cents)
When Your Family Goes Camping. Ralph Bugg (75 cents)

NATURE STUDY, CONSERVATION, AND ECOLOGY

Ecological Renewal, Paul E. Lutz and H. Paul Santmire. Fortress Press, Philadelphia, 1972 ($1.00).
Golden Nature Guides. Golden Press, Racine, Wis. ($1.00).

Birds	Mammals	Seashores
Fishes	Pond Life	Stars
Flowers	Reptiles and Amphibians	Trees
Fossils	Rocks and Minerals	Weather
Insects		

Handbook for Ecology Learning Centers, Edward L. Schlingman. DECEE, P.O. Box 179, St. Louis, MO 63166 ($1.95).
Living with Energy, Ronald Alves. Penguin Books, New York, 1978 ($7.95).
Silent Spring, Rachel Carson. Fawcett World Library, New York, 1975 ($1.75).
The Web of Life, John H. Storer. The New American Library, Inc., New York, 1972 ($1.25).

CRAFTS AND CREATIVE ACTIVITIES

Church Family Gatherings, Joe Leonard, Jr., ed. Judson Press, Valley Forge, 1978 ($4.95).
Clues to Creativity, M. Franklin and Maryann Dotts. Friendship Press, New York, Vol. 1, A-I ($3.95); Vol. 2, J-P ($3.95); Vol. 3, R-W ($4.50).
Creative Activities, Mabel Adcock and Elsie Blackwell. Warner Press, Inc., Anderson, Ind., 1964 ($2.50).
Native 'N' Creative, Thelma Stinson. United Methodist Church, Discipleship Resources, P.O. Box 840, Nashville, TN 37202 (40 cents).
Stepping Stones to Nature, Robert O. Bale. Burgess Publishing Company, Minneapolis, 1960 ($3.00).

RECREATION

Children's Games from Many Lands, Nina Millen. Friendship Press, New York, 1965 ($3.50).
Fun Encyclopedia, Elvin O. Harbin. Abingdon Press, Nashville ($8.95).

The New Pleasure Chest, Helen and Larry Eisenberg. Abingdon Press, Nashville, 1972 ($1.95).

The Recreation Job in Camp and Conference, Edward L. Schlingman. DECEE, P.O. Box 179, St. Louis, MO 63166 (50 cents).

MUSIC

Many denominations have prepared their own camp and conference songbook. Consult your headquarters.

Sing a Tune. Informal Music, Delaware, Ohio (30 cents).

The Whole World Singing. Friendship Press, New York, 1950, ($2.95).

MARRIAGE AND FAMILY ENRICHMENT

Black Families and the Struggle for Survival, Andrew Billingsley. Friendship Press, New York, 1974 ($1.95).

Cherishable: Love and Marriage, David W. Augsburger. Herald Press, Scottdale, Pa., 1971 ($1.50).

Christian Parenthood, Helen H. Sherrill. John Knox Press, Atlanta, 1964 ($2.45).

Christians in Families, Roy W. Fairchild. John Knox Press, Atlanta, 1964 ($3.25).

Family Problems and What to Do About Them, Wallace Denton. The Westminster Press, Philadelphia, 1971 ($4.50).

First of All Persons: A New Look at Men-Women Relationships, Elizabeth S. and William H. Genné. Friendship Press, New York, 1973 ($1.95).

Generations Learning Together, Donald and Patricia Griggs. Griggs Educational Service, 1731 Barcelona St., Livermore, CA 94550, 1976.

Great Days for the Family, Harold Belgum. Concordia Publishing House, St. Louis, 1969 ($3.95).

How to Have a Happy Marriage, David and Vera Mace. Abingdon Press, Nashville, 1977 ($6.95).

The Love-Fight, David W. Augsburger. Herald Press, Scottdale, Pa., 1973 ($1.65).

Love Happens in Families, Larry Harman, ed. Christian Family Movement, 1655 Jackson Blvd., Chicago, IL 60612, 1974.

Marriage and Family Enrichment: New Perspectives and Programs, Herbert A. Otto, ed. Abingdon Press, Nashville, 1976 ($6.95).

Raising Your Child, Not by Force But by Love, Sidney D. Craig. The Westminster Press, Philadelphia, 1973 ($5.95).

Sexual Problems in Marriage, F. Philip Rice. The Westminster Press, Philadelphia, 1978 ($6.95).

Young Black Adults: Liberation and Family Attitudes, George B. Thomas. Friendship Press, New York, 1974 ($1.95).

OLDER FAMILIES

Adventures with Older Adults in Outdoor Settings, George B. Ammon. United Church Press, New York, 1972 ($1.80).

Aging Is Not for Sissies, Terry Schuckman. The Westminster Press, Philadelphia, 1975 ($2.95).

Growing Old Is a Family Affair, Dorothy B. Fritz. The Westminster Press, Philadelphia, 1972 ($2.95).

Living Creatively as an Older Adult, Glenn H. Asquith. Herald Press, Scottdale, Pa., 1975 ($1.95).

Outdoor Education Programs with Older Adults: Seven Reports. National Council of Churches, Room 706, 475 Riverside Drive, New York, NY 10027, 1977 ($1.00).

WORSHIP AND BIBLE STUDY

The Bible Speaks to You, Robert M. Brown. The Westminster Press, Philadelphia, 1977 ($3.95).

Celebrate Summer: Guidebook for Families, Gabe Huck. Paulist Press, New York ($3.95).

Family Cluster Programs, R. Ted Nutting. Judson Press, Valley Forge, 1978 ($2.95).

Let Us Worship God: An Interpretation for Families, John F. Jansen. John Knox Press, Atlanta, 1967 ($2.45).

Let's Talk About God: Devotions for Families with Young Children, Gertrude Priester. The Westminster Press, Philadelphia, 1967 ($3.95).

Survival Prayers for Young Mothers, Deborah A. Holmes. John Knox Press, Atlanta, 1976 ($4.95).

FAMILIES WITH SPECIAL NEEDS

The National Council of Churches has prepared a very comprehensive list of resources for the mentally retarded, emotionally disturbed, visually handicapped, hearing impaired, physically and/or socially handicapped. Order *Resources for the Christian Education of Persons with Special Learning Needs* from the Office of Special Education, Room 708, 475 Riverside Drive, New York, NY 10027, for $1.00. Also available from the same address are: *Leisure Activities for Adults Who Are Retarded* (50 cents) and *Selected*

Resources on Human Sexuality and the Mentally Retarded (50 cents).

AUDIOVISUAL RESOURCES

Audio-Visual Resource Guide. Friendship Press, New York, 1976 ($8.95). This book lists and evaluates over 250 films and filmstrips under the heading "The Christian Family."

For family conferences, it is usually wise to have a few extra films on the wonder of nature or family life in case inclement weather forces the program to move indoors.

Appendixes

APPENDIX A

SCHEDULE OF PREPARATIONS

This schedule assumes a major event of approximately a week in duration. It is meant to serve as a step-by-step guide and checklist for committees sponsoring family camps or conferences and for the staffs which administer such events.

Twelve Months in Advance

Sponsoring committee
1. Decides purposes and type of program
2. Selects site and dates
3. Determines budget and costs
4. Selects a director-family and other staff families.

Nine Months in Advance

Sponsoring committee*
1. Releases publicity
2. Plans promotion campaign
3. Completes selection of staff.

Six Months in Advance

Sponsoring committee pushes promotion campaign. Staff
1. Develops letters, portrait sheets, etc., and begins correspondence as soon as families register.
2. Consults with site managment, clarifying their respective responsibilities.

*Once director-family is selected, continuous consultation is assumed.

Three Months in Advance

Sponsoring committee continues promotion of registrations. Staff
1. Corresponds with and gathers information from registrants.
2. Meets for inspection of site and preplanning.
3. Confirms staff responsibilities in writing.
4. Arranges for ordering program supplies.

One Month in Advance

Sponsoring committee promotes registrations. Staff
1. Begins to involve registrants in some special responsibilities (worship planning, recreational leadership, etc.) as interests and abilities are discovered.

One Week in Advance

Sponsoring committee consults with director-family on final details.

Director-family checks on details of all preceding planning.
1. Notifies staff of any late registrants.
2. Checks on arrival time of staff.

One or Two Days in Advance

Staff families arrive on site.

Opening Day

Staff families carry forward opening day plans.

Day Following Event

Staff families prepare their evaluations.

One Week After Event

Director-family submits summary of evaluations and recommendations to the sponsoring committee.

Sponsoring Committee
1. Cleans up all financial responsibilities for the event just past.
2. Receives recommendations from staff and campers and begins making plans for any future events.

APPENDIX B

SITE CHECKLIST

This list is for use of the sponsoring committee in selecting an adequate site in conformity with the standards of the Committee on Outdoor Education of the National Council of Churches and the American Camping Association. Committees interested in purchasing and developing a site of their own should get in touch with the site development consultant of their own denomination or of the NCC Committee on Outdoor Education.

Location   YES   NO

1. Is the site removed from populated areas and distracting resorts?   ☐   ☐

2. Is the site free from dangerous hazards and adequately drained?   ☐   ☐

3. Are there adequate natural resources and sufficient space for the type of program intended? (For a camping program, allow one acre per camper.)   ☐   ☐

Facilities

1. Are tents, cabins, or shelters in safe condition and constructed in accordance with the building codes of the locality? Are there adequate facilities for recreational vehicles?   ☐   ☐

2. Are there adequate buildings or shelter for program activities, even in inclement weather?   ☐   ☐

3. Are buildings heated for cool or damp weather?   ☐   ☐

4. Do sleeping accommodations allow complete privacy for each family unit?   ☐   ☐

5. Are doorways, doorhandles, drinking fountains, etc., accessible and safe for children?   ☐   ☐

6. Is there a safe play area for smaller children?   ☐   ☐

7. Are waterfront areas or swimming pools located, constructed, and equipped in compliance with applicable laws; or do they meet the standards of a recognized water safety agency, such as the YMCA, the American Camping Association, or the American Red Cross?   ☐   ☐

Food Service

1. Are water and milk supplies certified safe? □ □
2. Are there adequate refrigeration and other facilities for proper storage of food? □ □
3. Is the food preparation area adequate in size, clean, and protected from insects and rodents? □ □
4. Do dishwashing procedures and care of food equipment comply with local sanitary laws or meet approved practices? □ □
5. Is garbage and waste disposal handled in a manner approved by health officials? □ □

Health, Sanitation, and Safety

1. Do plumbing and sanitary facilities meet all applicable legal requirements? □ □
2. Is there an adequate supply of hot water? □ □
3. Is there a shower head for each fifteen campers or other facilities for bathing with warm water? □ □
4. Are there toilet facilities for both sexes? □ □
5. Is there a toilet seat for each ten campers? □ □
6. Are toilets clean and flyproof? □ □
7. Are there handwashing facilities near toilets? □ □
8. Is there a health center with facilities for isolating ill persons? □ □
9. Is there a nurse or doctor in attendance? (A doctor should always be available on call if a nurse is on the site.) □ □
10. Is emergency transportation always available? □ □

APPENDIX C

A TYPICAL LETTER FROM A DIRECTOR-FAMILY

(An earlier letter has been sent acknowledging the receipt of the registration fee, enclosing a "portrait sheet," and telling something about the director's family.)

Dear Folks:

It won't be long now! That is, not long till we all get together at Family Camp.

It will please all who have been at camp with them before to know that Sam and Tillie will be our Camp Naturalist and Nurse.

Just in case you haven't spent many nights in a well-ventilated cabin recently, don't forget Bill's suggestion to bring at least two blankets for each person. Each cabin has one convenience outlet in addition to the center light, in case your bedding is electrified.

Other things that sometimes come in handy are a few clothespins, raincoats, sand toys, a clipboard for sketching, scissors and old crayons for the "small fry," musical instruments, and hobby tools—including elementary woodworking tools (if you're not too particular about them), such as saw, hammer, plane, small square, and a rule or tape.

One of the things we like to do at Family Camp is for each family to make a sign to identify its cabin. It all helps to get acquainted and also gives a chance for a little originality if you want to make a play on your name, hometown, etc. You may want to dream up an idea for yours while en route or even make it at home. If so, we'd suggest using a piece of light cardboard not over 12" x16".

Old campers know we always have a "Family Fun Night" toward the end of camp. The most successful "acts" have been short skits put on by an entire family—or all members old enough to participate. A little advance notice may give you time to come up with one that will "bring down the house."

In case you want to leave your address with a friend, it's (post office address). *The telephone is* (phone number).

We'll be seeing you Sunday afternoon, August 22, between 2 and 4—in time to "set up housekeeping" in your cabin before dinner at 5:45—starting a week your family will long remember.

Sincerely,

P.S. Borrowing an idea from last year, we'd like to suggest that while en route to camp you make up words to fill in the blanks below. At dinner Sunday evening each family will get to sing its version. (Anyone who can't sing well can have more fun by singing LOUD!) Here 'tis—here's a sample to give you the idea—

> *Hi Ho! Hi Ho!*
> *It's off to camp we go;*
>
> _____ _____ _____ _____
>
> _____ _____ _____ _____
>
> *Hi Ho, Hi Ho!*
>
> *Hi Ho! Hi Ho!*
> *It's off to camp we go;*
> *We'll load our trunk*
> *With all our junk;*
> *Hi Ho, Hi Ho!*

APPENDIX D

A FAMILY PORTRAIT SHEET

Families enrolling for camp are asked to furnish information to assist the directors in their planning. The staff members are basically enablers to help all of us express our talents and our interests, and so you, too, will be involved in leading activities from time to time. In filling out this form, don't be so modest that you conceal your abilities.

Names of Couple _____ and _____ _____
                     (husband)   (wife)   (surname)

Name of Additional Adult _____ _____ Nickname _____

Names of Children	Age	Sex	Grade	Nickname
_____	_____	_____	_____	_____
_____	_____	_____	_____	_____
_____	_____	_____	_____	_____
_____	_____	_____	_____	_____
_____	_____	_____	_____	_____
_____	_____	_____	_____	_____

Father's Nickname _____ Occupation _____

    Hobbies or Interests _____

Mother's Nickname _____ Occupation _____

    Hobbies or Interests _____

This will be our _____ year in a family camp.

To help us get a clearer picture of your family's interests and skills, please write names in the blank spaces.

	Like to Learn	Like to Participate	Can Lead
Group Singing	_____	_____	_____
Folk Dancing	_____	_____	_____
Nature Study	_____	_____	_____
Crafts (specify)	_____	_____	_____
Sports (specify)	_____	_____	_____

List other interests of family members on the reverse side.
Special Needs:

Dietary or medical _____

Allergy _____

Restriction on activity _____

	Names
Have any of you had lifeguard experience?	_____
Have any of you had first-aid training?	_____
Have any of you had medical experience?	_____
Have any of you had leadership in Scouting?	_____
Have any of you taught Sunday School?	_____
Do any of you play piano or organ?	_____

NOTE: For a family conference with scheduled classes or discussion groups, the following additional information might be helpful.

In the parents' hour, which topics would you like to discuss?

_____What are the facts about normal child development?

_____How do children affect the husband-wife relationship?

_____What can we do about children's quarreling?

_____What is effective discipline?

Suggestions of other topics:

What would you like to discuss with the pastor?

_____How can we teach the Bible most helpfully?

_____What Christian beliefs are essential in family?

_____When is a family "Christian"?

Other suggestions: _____

Young people (seventh grade and older) are asked to number the following subjects in the order of their preference. These may be used in the morning discussions.

_____Does the Bible really help us today?

_____What difference do Christian beliefs make?

_____What should Christians believe?

_____Can prayer change things?

_____What makes a decision or act moral?

Suggestions of some other topics: _____

Please return this form as soon as possible.

APPENDIX E

A FAMILY COVENANT

OUR FAMILY CAMP Covenant
PILGRIM HAVEN · · AUG. 22-28, 1954

Recognizing that the experiences of WORK, PLAY, LOVE and WORSHIP are common to our family living, we covenant with God and one another to endeavor to enrich these areas of our family life.

To accept WORK in paid employment, in home, school, church and community tasks as an opportunity for personal growth.

To participate in PLAY out of which will come true sportsmanship, real relaxation, personal and family enjoyment.

To cultivate LOVE in such a way that it becomes the expression of our concern for others.

To engage in WORSHIP as a means of expressing our gratitude to God for his gifts, and our commitment to his way of life as revealed by Jesus Christ.